GW00360311

FIND YOUR
LIFE PATH

First published in Great Britain in 2024 by
Michael O'Mara Books Limited
9 Lion Yard
Tremadoc Road
London SW4 7NQ

Copyright © Michael O'Mara Books Limited 2024
Illustrations © Anna Stead licensed by Jehane Ltd 2024

All rights reserved. You may not copy, store, distribute, transmit, reproduce or otherwise make available this publication (or any part of it) in any form, or by any means (electronic, digital, optical, mechanical, photocopying, recording or otherwise), without the prior written permission of the publisher. Any person who does any unauthorized act in relation to this publication may be liable to criminal prosecution and civil claims for damages.

A CIP catalogue record for this book is available from the British Library.

This product is made of material from well-managed, FSC®-certified forests and other controlled sources. The manufacturing processes conform to the environmental regulations of the country of origin.

ISBN: 978-1-78929-598-6 in paperback print format
ISBN: 978-1-78929-599-3 in ebook format

1 2 3 4 5 6 7 8 9 10

Cover design by Natasha Le Coultre
using illustrations by Anna Stead, licensed by Jehane Ltd
Designed by Natasha Le Coultre and Barbara Ward

Printed and bound in China

www.mombooks.com

MIX
Paper | Supporting
responsible forestry
FSC® C010256

FSC
www.fsc.org

FIND YOUR LIFE PATH

Chart Your Destiny with the Magic of
NUMEROLOGY

Written by
CAROLYNE FAULKNER

Illustrated by
ANNA STEAD

Michael O'Mara Books Limited

Contents

Introduction: What is Numerology?   7

Pythagorean Numerology   12

Soul Numbers   28

Growth Numbers   38

Astrological Numerology   48

Life Path Numbers   61

Life Path Master Numbers   80

Angel Numbers   88

Angel Numbers and Their Archangels   92

Birthday Numbers   111

Communicating With Your Higher Self   126

Introduction:
What is Numerology?

In a world full of uncertainty, you can always count on numbers. Sacred numerological sequences, otherwise known as numerology, are a way of interpreting the hidden messages behind numbers. Scientific genius and innovator Nikola Tesla became obsessed with the numbers 3, 6 and 9, believing them to hold the key to mysteries of the universe, but unfortunately he took those secrets to the grave. The practice of assigning mystical meaning to specific numbers dates as far back as the eighth century BC. We do know that numbers and numerology can unlock our own potential, and this book is a great place to begin!

In order to see how our seemingly spontaneous and chaotic universe has formed and continues to develop using a very precise and orderly system, you only need to take a leaf from the book of nature and the most famous numerical series of all: the Fibonacci sequence. These numbers describe the patterns that appear in flowers, seashells, tornadoes and throughout the spiralling galaxies of space, operating in cycles that can be deciphered on many levels.

There are a few different ways to approach numerology. Pythagorean numerology, or modern numerology as it is sometimes called, uses the alphabet to discern your life path number, as well as other key numbers from your name. If you favour this method and your language doesn't use the Latin alphabet, there are numerous websites that can help you calculate your numbers, and I've also included a simple exercise to help you decipher these for yourself. Soul numbers

– those that summarize the qualities you already possess – use only the vowels in your name. Growth numbers, on the other hand, are calculated using only the letters in your first name or your nickname, and these indicate how best to grow and evolve in your life.

Astrological numerology, meanwhile, focuses on your date of birth and other specific dates and numbers that indicate messages from the universe. In this book we'll explore angel numbers and the important messages such numbers hold. We'll also explore my unique practice of assigning actual angels and archangels to angel numbers. The idea for this is rooted in ancient scriptures. I often use it with my clients to help reveal more about their destiny and life path.

I also refer to 'vibrations' throughout this book. For those of you who may not be familiar with the term, a vibration is an energy. A high vibe, for example, is held by someone with a positive mindset and attitude. This energy can also be felt around us – a room may have a good vibe, meaning it makes you feel good to be there, or a negative one that causes you to feel a bit low. Reading vibes is spiritual and can be a way of training our intuition.

As you acquaint yourself with this beautifully illustrated book, the order behind the main methods in numerology will be revealed to you. These steps have been presented in a condensed form, to enable you to fast-track your knowledge of the art. I have provided exercises to help train you to trust your own intuition, chart your life path and read the messages from the universe. I also offer mantras throughout the book and these should be read out loud and repeated several times so that the words resonate on a heartfelt level and touch your soul. Memorize the mantras that chime with you and take them with you into your daily life.

It's helpful to use a journal alongside this book to note down your findings, to record any insights that may pop up and to use for the gratitude exercises listed. Numerology is an art not a science, and there's an implicit intelligence in the universe, or a higher power that you work with when you tune into your own intuition. Choosing between the numbers you use is a creative exercise that aligns you with the divine meaning that resonates most for you.

You may read this book from cover to cover to familiarize yourself with numerology and take part in the exercises, or you may use it intuitively by opening a random page and seeing what awaits you inside.

May you find inspiration, meaning and guidance in the pages that follow.

Pythagorean Numerology

Pythagoras was an ancient Greek mystic, mathematician and philosopher. He believed in the vibrational energy of certain numbers and that every letter in the alphabet had a particular numerical value. If your language doesn't use the Latin alphabet but you wish to use this method, you can find a simple technique below that works. There are also many websites and apps that can be used to determine your 'core' numbers in other alphabets.

Pythagorean numerology switches letters for numbers. Each letter is aligned with a number, and these numbers are then added together to give you a single number that conveys a message from the universe. If the numbers add up to over 10, you add the numbers that make up that number together until you are left with a single digit. The exception to this is 11 or 22 and, in some cases, 33, as these are all master numbers and therefore not to be separated – they have their own powerful, standalone meaning.

So, for example, if your name is Marie Anne James:

$$M = 4, A = 1, R = 9, I = 9, E = 5$$

Add them all together and you have 28. Reduce this to one digit by adding them together to give you 10, then reduce again to 1 by adding 1 to 0.

If you just use your first name, this is your growth number (see page 38), but to calculate your full Pythagorean number (and life path number, see page 61) you'd need to calculate your numbers using your whole name.

You might also like to create your own version of the Pythagorean table if you are a non-Latin-alphabet user – it's easy and can also be fun!

To determine the value or number associated with each letter in any language, write out the letters of your alphabet in chronological order and band them into rows of nine each.

Each letter has a value. For example, the first group of letters is valued as 1, the second group is 2 and so on until you get to 9.

Master Numbers

As well as being incredibly powerful, it is also believed that master numbers portray the key stages of evolutionary creation. For example, 11 is an extremely high vibrational number, meaning that it resonates with a high frequency and has the capacity to alter negativity into light. It also indicates a person with visionary capabilities. If it appears as a reoccurring number, it is a sign that a visionary message is on its way to you. These signs indicate the importance of finding your deeper purpose and are about encouraging an awareness that awakens you from inertia.

The master numbers 11, 22 and 33 often have more power than other numbers. We are being asked to raise our vibrations and become more conscious and conscientious as a race. We can do this by becoming less consumeristic and more positive and grateful beings, which serves the planet and helps with the paradigm shift towards a more ideal society. On a personal note, the more loving and positive you are, the more like-minded people will gravitate towards you and enhance your experience of daily life.

— ∘ ∘ Core Numbers ∘ ∘ —

Core numbers stay with you throughout your life and derive from your date of birth and the name you were given at birth, so they do not change.

— ∘ ∘ Dynamic Numbers ∘ ∘ —

These are numbers that alter, such as your growth number, angel numbers and your soul number, which would be used if your name changed at any stage in your life.

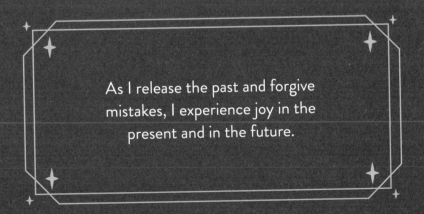

As I release the past and forgive mistakes, I experience joy in the present and in the future.

'Numbers rule the universe.'

PYTHAGORAS

The Meaning of Pythagorean Numbers

1

You have the ability to become a leader if you so wish. This could be on a grand scale or without ego, but you always set the best example and motivate others to become the best versions of themselves, too.

2

You have the innate ability to overcome worldly desires and to create a life with meaning no matter how humble your circumstances may be. You have good values and morals and always support others if they are less fortunate or have talent that requires nurturing.

Exercise: developing self-love

Take a few moments to reflect on the conversations you have with yourself. Are they kind and loving? If so, great! Carry on as you are and inspire others to operate in the same way. If not, make a promise to your soul that you will become more compassionate towards yourself. Note how this promise makes you feel.

Try to monitor how you feel when you are self-critical, as opposed to being kind to yourself. Isn't the difference vast?

Living with regret for past mistakes only creates sadness. Write down any perceived mistakes you've made in the past, or regrets you still carry around. Then burn that note (safely) and use this ritual to begin to let it go.

List some things that make you the special being you are. These could be your kindness, an open, loving heart, or your general willingness to help others.

3

You are learning through your achievements and failures. This number is thought not only to be lucky but also to bestow wisdom. Juggling too many things and not finishing projects, however, can be an issue. It's important that you learn, listen and use the lessons of the past to move forward with grace and optimism.

4

You are security-conscious and cautious, which may hold you back from experiencing enlightening opportunities. You usually have a great work ethic, seeking to create wealth and, in some cases, status. Stability can only really be found in one's own mind – for those who have a higher faith in the universe and its benevolence, there is strength.

5

You are known as the adventurer, with a spirit of curiosity that is inspiring. You are usually extremely social but may be overly opportunistic. Your need for change can either help you grow or cause you to become bored quickly. Recognizing how those around you contribute to your life increases contentment.

6

You are usually in a position to attract good fortune, stability and security, although you may become miserly if you feel insecure. A lovely home and the finer things in life are important for you, but you almost always create your own fortune and working hard to achieve these things is the best course of action.

7

You are often spiritually curious, and this number is thought to be extremely powerful in many religions. On a quest to find deeper meaning in life, the ordinary nature of daily life often feels frustrating for you. But there is calmness and security to be found in the mundane, and spending time alone helps you heal and replenish.

8

You prefer to be in control of your own destiny and can be unforgiving. Your lesson in life is to learn gentleness and kindness. You can be overly materialistic and concerned with your own ambitions. Understanding and empathy for self and others will enable you to overcome emotional blockages and embrace the joys of life.

9

You are a born philosopher and are happiest when you feel as if you are helping in some way. You follow your dreams and hold the potential to actually achieve them. You must be careful not to overindulge in fantasy and to face your fears rather than using distraction techniques, which you have down to an art form.

11

You are the visionary number and often have the ability to draw on the higher consciousness of the universe. This provides you with great insight, so that you may guide and counsel others wisely. Meditation and learning how to quieten your mind will give you deeper understanding of your true purpose in this life.

22

You are the pioneering number and have the ability to make major plans and execute them where others may falter. Other people are drawn to you and are often willing to support your goals, which need to be altruistic for the very best results. Working with the law of gratitude, which means actively seeking out and appreciating all the blessings you already have, will help you attract and achieve more than you ever dreamed of.

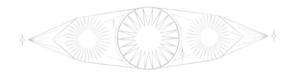

33

You are the seeker's number, without ego. This means you have a thirst for knowledge and a desire to unlock the secrets of life, which may have sent you to the far-flung corners of the world in search of truth. What you have learned, you are destined to share in some way.

Exercise: cultivating gratitude

Gratitude is like a magnet – when we show appreciation, the universe sends us even more to be grateful for.

1. Make your own piece of art featuring the word 'Gratitude'. It could be a collage, a drawing or simply the words in black on white paper. Now place it somewhere you can see it every morning.

2. As you stand in front of your creation, think of three people who bring joy to your life and thank the universe for bringing them in.

3. Start a gratitude journal and add to it each day, even when you feel less than grateful! List the things you are grateful for. Start with small blessings and build up.

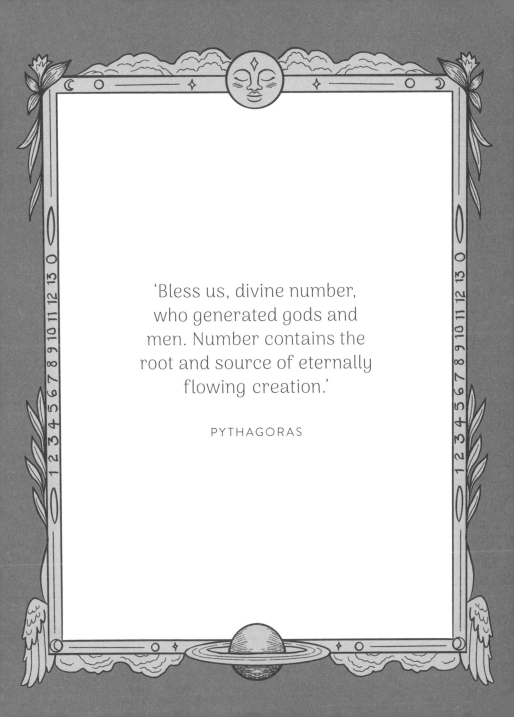

'Bless us, divine number,
who generated gods and
men. Number contains the
root and source of eternally
flowing creation.'

PYTHAGORAS

Soul Numbers

Soul numbers are usually calculated using the Pythagorean table but only use the number of vowels in your full birth name. If you have changed your name, try calculating both and see which number and its guidance resonates for you most.

You might like to simply count the numbers of your whole birth name which leads to your growth number; again try both and see which works better for you when reading the insights.

So, for example: if your name is Jon, there is only one vowel here. So, you could read about the number 1, but you could also use the Pythagorean method which gives the letter O the value of 6. Feel free to read them both and see which one resonates most.

These numbers reveal the qualities you already innately possess and indicate tips and guidance from your soul. They can help soothe and assist you in life if you adhere to the helpful messages associated with them while avoiding worldly cravings. Too much attachment to anything external causes us much suffering, and aversion to working on ourselves can lead us to run from the lessons life is pushing us to learn. Soul numbers ask us to 'lean in' — to persevere and accept challenges head-on.

1

Overcoming anger and obstacles with a happy heart and the spirit of compromise.

Avoid being overly competitive or a show-off.

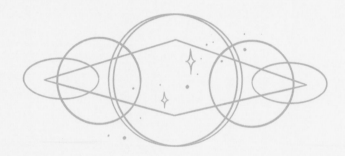

2

Developing the right set of values and stepping away from an overly consumeristic lifestyle.

Avoid being too defensive and closing your heart due to fear.

3

Communicating with yourself and others with love in your heart, and being honest with yourself and truthful with others.

Avoid being flaky and demonstrating a lack of commitment due to the fear of missing out (FOMO).

4

Cultivating emotional intelligence and a spiritual outlook that accepts what has been and forges a more grateful way forward.

Avoid failing to recognize other people's contributions or using others for personal gain.

5

Living a more creative life that allows your passions to free-flow. Understanding the creative process and respecting the value it brings to your own life and those around you.

Avoid being deceitful and hedging your bets in life.

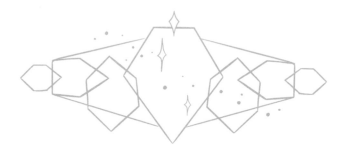

6

Letting go of the need to control every aspect of life and trusting more in the divine plan and timing of the universe.

Avoid resentment in any form and leave the past behind.

Exercise: attracting prosperity

1. Sit quietly with your legs crossed and your back supported. Breathe deeply several times.

2. Ask yourself what prosperity means for you. Now visualize what you really want in life and allow the images to flood your senses.

3. Write down all your wishes and cross out any that you honestly know are not good for your spiritual life.

4. Now ask yourself if your desires align with your soul. Are they really good for you in the long term? Thank the universe for granting your wishes.

7

Seeking knowledge and wisdom through philosophical and spiritual works. Sharing what you have learned with others in ways that help them to grow too.

Avoid becoming too isolated or critical of humanity in general.

8

Achieving power and status in life and then using it wisely in ways that benefit others by ensuring that the power we gain does not cause harm.

Avoid being ruthless or detached from your natural sense of compassion.

9

Benefiting humanity in some way that also uses creativity and using your innate enthusiasm and ability to inspire others to bring about change.

Avoid becoming intolerant or elitist.

11

Sharing ideas and thoughts with others in ways that deepen their understanding of the spiritual realms. Seeing difficult times as opportunities to grow.

Avoid self-pity or negative thoughts and self-talk.

22

Standing in your strength, perhaps to carry out a predestined mission. This mission could simply be about becoming a better version of yourself, or it could involve ideas and inspiration that help raise the vibration of the planet in some way.

Avoid becoming consumed with the small things that don't matter.

33

Surrendering to the intelligence of the universe and trusting in the directions you are given. Operating with a high vibration that isn't swayed too much by worldly concerns.

Avoid feeling lonely or spending time with people from the Low Vibe Tribe.

Exercise: my vibe attracts my soul tribe

Take note of the friends and colleagues you spend most time with.

Are they positive? Kind? Inspirational? If so, congratulations! You are a member of the High Vibe Tribe. If not, it's time to make moves!

Attend classes that focus on healing – this will help you rise.

Sign up to spiritual teachings you are drawn to.

Slowly detach from negative relationships as much as you can and ask the universe to send you friends and connections with higher vibrations.

Growth Numbers

Simply put, growth numbers help you to grow and advance through your life's journey. They reveal the skills we should dial into so that we can navigate our own paths through the rhythms of our lives.

Your growth number is calculated from your first name or your nickname, you simply count the letters to get to your number. You may use the system created by Pythagoras, which uses the alphabet, or simply add the number of letters in your name to find your growth number.

In addition to this, you can dig a little deeper by taking your growth number and adding to it today's date to discover your progress number. This signifies how far you have come throughout life's journey, what you are destined to learn and how best to grow.

If, for example, your growth number is 6, to get your progress number you would need to add 6 to the date, or you may simply use the year.

If today is 9 February 2024, the calculation would be: 9 + 2 (for the second month of the year) = 11 + 20 + 24 = 55. This needs to be reduced to a single digit, so we add 5 + 5 together to get 10 and then take that down to 1, because 1 + 0 = 1.

If we then add 1 to your original growth number, we discover that your progress number is 7.

To calculate your progress number for the year, you simply add the year to your growth number, for example 2024 = 2 + 0 + 2 + 4 = 8, and then using the growth number 6: 6 + 8 = 14, reducing that to a single digit 1 + 4 = 5, which is your progress number for the year.

You can then read up on your number in the following pages to gauge the level you have reached in the spiritual story of your life so far. The calculations for different years will change and give you a new read; it may be interesting to review the progress numbers for past years and see how far you have come!

1

Expressing yourself without fear, spending time getting to know yourself through meditation, prayer and spirituality.

2

Developing a strong moral compass, examining your belief system and building your confidence and self-esteem.

3

Training your mind to become positive and learning the art of open and heartfelt communication.

Exercise: strengthening your moral compass

Being honest helps build unions and creates the opportunity for real intimacy. Try telling the truth for a whole day. It sounds easy, but we often fear honesty will lead us to lose something or someone, finding it easier to tell people what we think they want to hear.

Before you make a phone call, send a text or email, stop and recite the following:

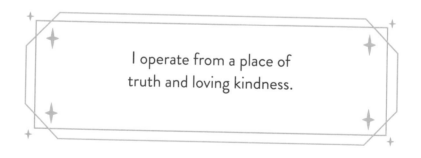

I operate from a place of
truth and loving kindness.

Truth helps us to become stronger and trusted. Write down one example of when you felt you had to lie. Now think about the situations that followed on from this lie – were there any? Were they good or bad? How did being dishonest make you feel?

Now do the same with an example of a time when you expressed yourself honestly, even though it was hard in that particular situation. How did that work out? How did it make you feel?

4

Overcoming insecurity and a lack of self-worth by becoming self-reliant and resourceful.

5

Using life lessons and experiences to make you stronger as opposed to resorting to blaming others.

6

Trusting yourself and removing anything that is out of alignment with your deeper purpose.

How to amplify
your inner power

Slow down, say less. Sometimes the more you speak, the less empowered you feel.

✦

Try to recall times when you have overshared with people who have not earned your trust. Did you feel exposed? If yes, try to bear this in mind for the future.

✦

Being too open, too soon, is disempowering. Try to imagine yourself wearing a mask, and only remove it when you feel safe.

✦

Take a break from social media and think about how often you overshare. Remove any posts that make you feel disempowered.

7

Developing your spiritual practice to align with a higher vision or purpose.

8

Learning how to handle power (your own and other people's) and money in ways that are fair, just and honest.

9

Cultivating compassion and kindness and operating in truthful ways that inspire others.

11

Looking deeper into what is presented and seeing through the veil many people hide behind to obscure their true nature.

22

Developing a strong faith in the power of the universe and your own courage, as well as cultivating insight and intuition.

33

Helping other people when needed and using your power to serve, which will bring your soul joy.

Astrological Numerology

In astrology, everything is banded into three. Three represents communication, or the storyteller, and astrology and numerology are ways to tell the story of you.

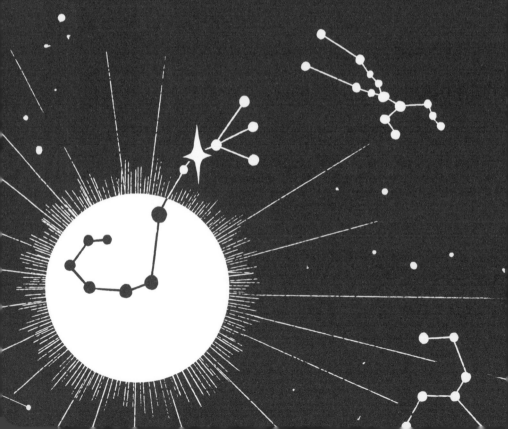

For example, when you're learning astrology, three is the magic number of signs – you study your rising sign, your moon sign and your sun sign (also known as the star sign). When looking at your natal chart (also known as a birth chart), you study the planet, the zodiac signs the planet falls in, and then the house it falls in. The planet represents 'what' that means for you, the sign is 'how' that manifests for good or not so good, and the house is 'where' that plays out for you in your life.

Astrology is a way to interpret your own characteristics and challenges, as well as the patterns and energy of the past, present and future. You may use your birth date, any significant numbers you are seeing, or the date of the day or a significant event to decipher the message.

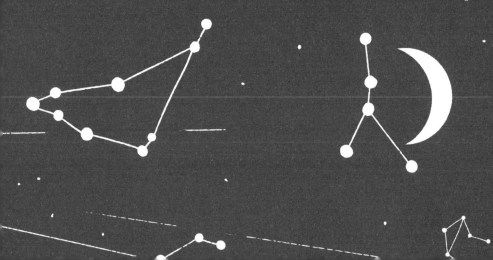

If you wish to use astrological numerology, the numbers we use are 1 to 12 as each of these represent a sign of the zodiac.

To find your astrological number, you simply add up the numbers in your full date of birth. You may also use this method to gain your number for the day and see which sign and message resonates for that particular day. Bring them to a single number unless it's a 10, 11 or 12, because in astrology we use the numbers 1 to 12.

For example, if you wanted to work out your number of the day for today, you'd take today's date – let's say it is 7 March 2023. We show this as 7 + 3 + 2 + 0 + 2 + 3 = 17. Taken down to one number, that's 8. So, your astrological number for the day is 8.

Exercise: morning ritual

Slow down with meditation.

1. Try five minutes to begin with and increase every day. Sit quietly, somewhere peaceful and uninterrupted.

2. Set an alarm for the time and take deep breaths until you become calm.

3. When a thought arises, breathe deeply, and don't give it additional energy. Keep the mind still. Let it go!

Aries: Number 1

This number is a message from the universe about self. Check how you may be presenting yourself, perhaps being too self-centred or on the other end of that not taking good enough care of number one, i.e. you. Number one also represents trusting your own instincts. Perhaps you need to defend your beliefs and be brave?

Taurus: Number 2

This is a message about material assets, self-worth and beliefs. You may be opening up to new ways of accruing wealth but be mindful not to associate money with self-worth. This may also be a message to check that your beliefs are positive and helping you to progress and grow spiritually.

Gemini: Number 3

This is a message to quieten the chatter of your mind, breathe deeply and listen to the subtle whispers of your soul or intuition. This could also be encouraging you to seek knowledge before making major decisions. Communication could be coming to you that is good news and poignant for your soul's journey.

Cancer: Number 4

This is a message to focus on your emotional intelligence and to stay calm, come what may. You may be overly reactive – instead step into your warrior energy and keep an open heart to others instead of taking things too personally or becoming defensive.

Exercise: a celebration ritual

1. Write a celebration list of at least two things to celebrate every morning.

2. Set an intention for the day. An example could be, 'Today I celebrate being alive' or 'I celebrate being loved'. Sit quietly and ponder your intention for a few moments.

3. Screenshot your list and make it your daily screen saver on your phone or computer, so that you'll be reminded of your things to celebrate throughout the day.

4. Take that joy with you into each day. Every time you feel depleted in any way, recite your list again. Note how uplifted you feel!

Leo: Number 5

This is a message of love. You can bring more love into your life by being loving and sidestepping ego. Stand in your light and shine without the need for external validation and find ways to bring the technicolour of creativity into your existence.

Virgo: Number 6

This is a message of health and healing. You are being sent healing vibes from the universe and may need to alter your daily routine so that it is healthier and less harmful. Avoid criticism, your own and other people's, as it lowers your vibration and blocks spirituality.

Libra: Number 7

This is a message of harmony and balance in all your relationships; perhaps arguments have prevented any real progress. Take this as a sign that the hearts of those involved are being opened and healed. If you have been struggling with your partner or wish for one, vow to attract balanced unions that sustain the test of time.

Scorpio: Number 8

This is a message of transformation and empowerment. Have patience because there are hidden factors still to be revealed. Avoid paranoia, trust yourself and develop your confidence in that respect by making decisions based on your gut instincts. Empower yourself!

Sagittarius: Number 9

This is a message of faith and inspiration. Take plenty of walks and hikes, as being outdoors in nature gives you a better connection to source energy (that is, energy from the universe) and sends in creative solutions. Spiritual studies such as meditation, yoga and Qigong are also well-starred for you, as they nourish your thirsty mind and heal your body.

Capricorn: Number 10

This is a message of kindness and compassion. Perhaps you are too hard on yourself and place too much onus on success, however that looks for you. Now is the time to release harsh self-judgements and to be kind and loving to yourself and others. Don't let failure harden you – instead thank the universe for the opportunity to learn.

Aquarius: Number 11

This is a message of awareness, to slow down and take a look at what's happening around you. Pay attention to signs and symbols as they are ways of guiding you and boosting confidence in the decisions you make. Be aware of the suffering of others and make moves to help where you can.

Pisces: Number 12

This is a message to release anything or anyone that is harmful to your more sensitive nature. Purify your life, however that looks, and allow generosity to feed and nourish your soul. Unleash your inner artist and begin to create the life you really want; visualization is always the first step.

Exercise: clarity and calm

1. Tap your forehead (third eye) several times with your two middle fingers and pause.

2. Breathe deeply and release any internal chatter causing you anxiety.

3. Repeat the exercise several times until calm washes over you.

4. When clarity takes over, thank the universe and repeat the exercise whenever you feel stressed or anxious – it's so powerful!

Life Path Numbers

Your life path number, or LPN for short, is one of the core numbers that stays with you throughout your life. It's reached by adding all the numbers of your birth date together to create a single digit and the practice dates back to ancient Babylon. The Babylonians used this method to divine the type of person you are destined to become. It is believed that your LPN emits a powerful vibration that reveals who you are, what you are best at doing, and also indicates innate talents that ought to be used in this lifetime. The LPN's calculation differs from the Pythagorean way of using the alphabet to determine the results.

To calculate your LPN you must first reduce the month, the day and then the year of your birth into a single number.

So if you were born on 7 August 1992, the sum would go like this:

$$7 + 8 + 1 + 9 + 9 + 2 = 36$$

Reduce this to one number by adding

$$3 + 6$$

and your LPN is 9.

This differs if you were born in November as it's the eleventh month and is a master number, so that remains as 11.

For example, if your birthday was 10 November 2002, the sum would go like this:

$$10 \text{ (day = 1)} + 11 \text{ (month = 11)} + 2 + 0 + 0 + 2 \text{ (year = 4)} = 16$$

Reduce this to one single digit and your LPN is 7.

'Numerology will help you
become more aware.'

ANKUR SRIVASTAVA

1

With this life path number, you have the ability to become a leader if you so wish. This may be on a grand scale or something quieter, without ego. It means that you have the ability to set the best example at all times and the power to motivate others to become the best versions of themselves too. You may make many promises, however, so be mindful not to overcommit until you know you can keep them.

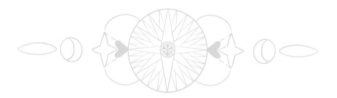

2

If your life path number is 2, this signifies that you have the innate ability to overcome worldly desires and to create a life with meaning, no matter how humble your circumstances may be. You will develop good values and morals and always support others less fortunate than you, as well as those who have talent that requires nurturing.

I will keep my promises, to myself and others.

✦

Keeping my word gives me the strength
to lead by example.

✦

I will only speak kindly to myself
and others today.

✦

I am a good person with true morals
and integrity.

✦

I will make my life one of meaning.

✦

I shall help those less fortunate,
as others help me.

Exercise: cultivating generosity

This exercise is designed to help you reflect on your good fortune and give back daily.

Make someone else's wellbeing your priority. This might be through giving your seat up to someone who needs it more on public transport, donating to a charity, buying a hot drink for a homeless person, or complimenting someone you see who has made an effort in some way.

How do these acts of kindness make you feel? In what parts of your life do you feel a show of kindness would be most effective? What motivates you to be kind?

Take the time to note these feelings down, so you can read this back to yourself at a later date and remind yourself of how good it felt to think of others. Trust that the universe always returns kindness to you in some form.

3

With this life path number, you are destined to become a brilliant communicator with the ability to intuit important messages from the universe and to inspire others. You are usually an extremely social person with a varied collection of interests and friends who trust you to do the right thing. You are also destined to become a peacemaker when misunderstandings or quarrels arise, and a messenger between the universe and those around you. In your desire to communicate, do beware of overtalking and try to listen more.

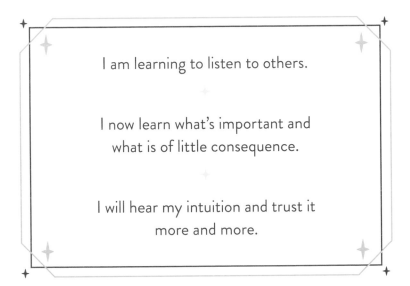

I am learning to listen to others.

I now learn what's important and what is of little consequence.

I will hear my intuition and trust it more and more.

Exercise: setting powerful intentions

The universe is asking us to take extra care of Mother Earth at the moment, and her health directly correlates with our own wellbeing.

Think about the amount you consume and vow to reduce your carbon footprint.

Take little, courageous steps forward, and have faith that they make a difference.

I know I have the power to make a difference.

I will go meat-free and/or fish-free for five days of the week, reduce my dairy intake and eat more plants.

I will try to buy local, and stop buying so many shipped items.

I will visit pre-loved clothing stores.

I will use my own reusable cup when buying hot drinks.

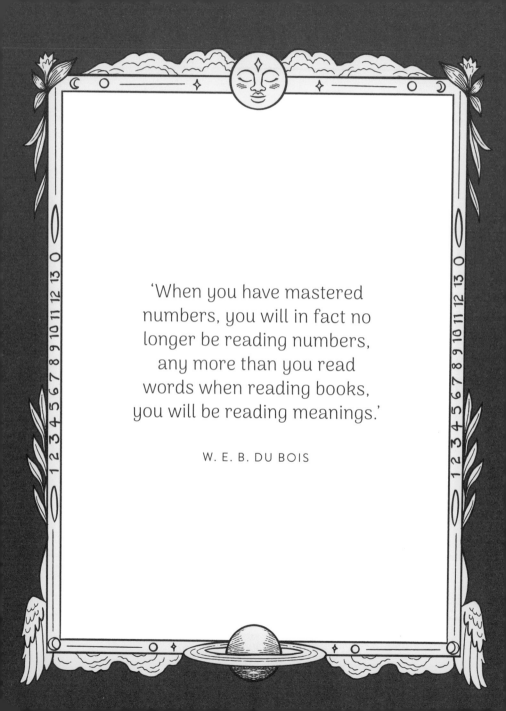

'When you have mastered numbers, you will in fact no longer be reading numbers, any more than you read words when reading books, you will be reading meanings.'

W. E. B. DU BOIS

Exercise: receiving messages from the universe

Sit with your life path number, take deep breaths, and allow any messages and images to flood in. Make a note in your journal of what you see and feel.

4

Your life path is intrinsically linked to honest endeavours, and you will have the tenacity and pragmatism to get things done and achieve major goals with integrity. Creativity and patience are skills that are innate but may need cultivation. Learning a musical instrument, or taking a class in creative writing or life drawing will reactivate your innate abilities. You can be risk averse, which can sometimes prevent you from experiencing the magic found in spontaneity.

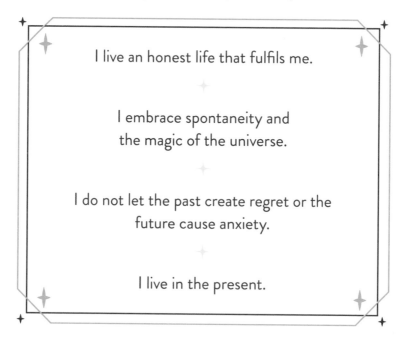

I live an honest life that fulfils me.

I embrace spontaneity and
the magic of the universe.

I do not let the past create regret or the
future cause anxiety.

I live in the present.

5

With this life path number, you live for adventure and need to solidify ideas to gain direction. You have the ability to rally others to a cause, or to your aid, but you must be wary of your own impatience and temper. You are destined to achieve a great many things but try to finish what you begin and stay firm in your convictions. Giving back will reward you whenever you may feel lost.

6

You are a great advisor, and you are likely to be organized and trustworthy and have usually assumed important responsibilities from a young age. Be mindful of being too serious in life and of simply going through the motions. Your life holds much potential to be of service to others, which ensures you good karma for this life and the next one. Avoiding criticism and remaining optimistic is the best way to enjoy your life and to embrace the gifts life has to offer.

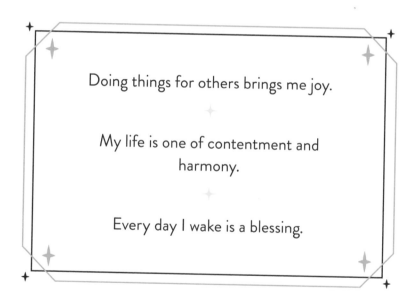

Doing things for others brings me joy.

My life is one of contentment and harmony.

Every day I wake is a blessing.

Exercise: tips for wellbeing

Make a pact with yourself to do more for your wellbeing
and inspire others to do the same along the way.

Unplug from anything digital for at least one hour
a day: this includes the television, your phone, etc.

Sit with yourself quietly, take deep, rejuvenating breaths
and perhaps recite your mantra. Take note of how this
makes you feel.

Try to make time for a walk without your phone and
concentrate on the fresh air and sounds around you.
Allow them to fill your whole being.

Smile at those who pass you by and don't expect
anything in return, just give!

7

You are charming and likely possess a brilliant and analytical mind. You may suffer from indecisiveness, so meditation and other mind-training practices will help you to become the great being you were destined to be. 'Born wise' is often a phrase used for those born under 7 as a life path number. Be mindful of over-the-top expectations of self and others and try to be more accepting of what is.

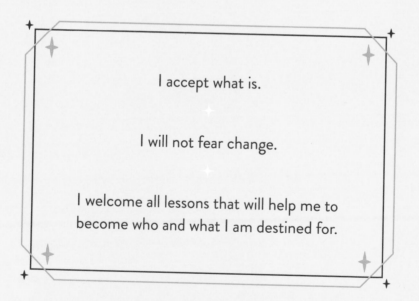

I accept what is.

I will not fear change.

I welcome all lessons that will help me to become who and what I am destined for.

8

With 8 as your life path number, you are destined to become important in the field you choose. You have the ability to bend others to your will. You also have a talent for manifesting material wealth should you wish, but this comes with a warning to constantly learn what's important. Use your power as a force for good because the law of cause and effect acts quickly for you, bringing back what you put out rapidly.

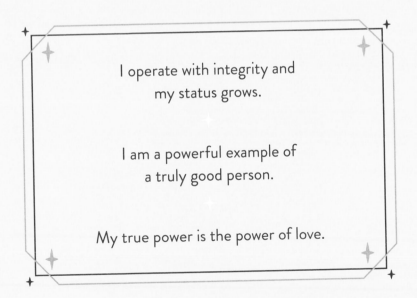

I operate with integrity and
my status grows.

I am a powerful example of
a truly good person.

My true power is the power of love.

9

This life path number belongs to those who excel in the world of words and prose. Usually, this means skilled writers and storytellers who have much to share with the world after they have studied and mastered their art, whichever form that takes. Those who are number 9 are often smart and kind – but beware of hiding your light under a bushel.

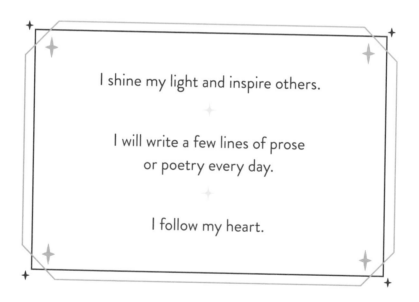

I shine my light and inspire others.

I will write a few lines of prose
or poetry every day.

I follow my heart.

'Wherever there is number,
there is beauty.'

PROCLUS

Life Path
Master Numbers

11

If this is your number, you have incredible insight and ideas that could even be described as ingenious. Your imagination has the power to set you free from any restrictions or problems you may face. You may have a strong intuition, which will grow as you develop it. The only potential drawbacks of this number are a lack of common sense and lacking the will to finish what you start, so grounding is vital for you to achieve your destiny if you're an 11.

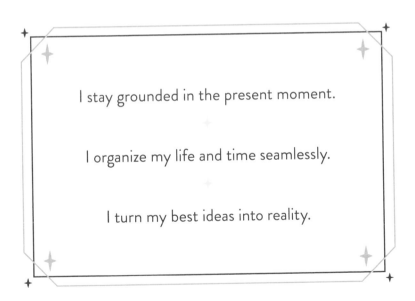

I stay grounded in the present moment.

I organize my life and time seamlessly.

I turn my best ideas into reality.

Exercise: working with master numbers

You can work with the high vibration of master numbers even if they aren't revealed as your actual life path number. You will need a pen and paper for this exercise.

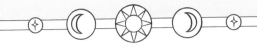

1. Focus on one of the following numbers and see which one resonates most: 11, 22 or 33.

2. Close your eyes and take deep, rejuvenating breaths. Place your hands on your heart and ask for the number to reveal something that serves your soul and your true purpose here on Earth.

3. Note the first image, symbol or word that comes to mind.

4. If you require further insight, stay in a calm space, breathe and gently ask again. It takes time to connect if you are used to working with only logic.

5. Make a note of anything that comes to mind, however random it seems in this moment, as it may become clear as the days progress.

22

With this as your life path number, you have the ability to merge wisdom with ancient knowledge and to use it in the modern world. You are a true visionary and innovator who may become known and respected in your field of choice, should you wish. You are talented and usually blend yin (feminine energy) and yang (masculine energy) seamlessly in all you do. The divine feminine and masculine are not about gender, and we all contain a combination of both. Beware of daydreaming and avoiding the real world, where you are needed.

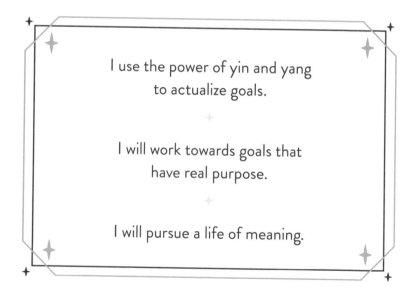

I use the power of yin and yang
to actualize goals.

I will work towards goals that
have real purpose.

I will pursue a life of meaning.

33

With this number, you are likely to be as skilled as an architect and have the ability to achieve what others wouldn't even dare to imagine. Support from others comes readily to you, and knowledge flows through your being. Beware of your own ego getting in the way and make plans that are fair to all. Use your abilities wisely and try not to become too self-indulgent.

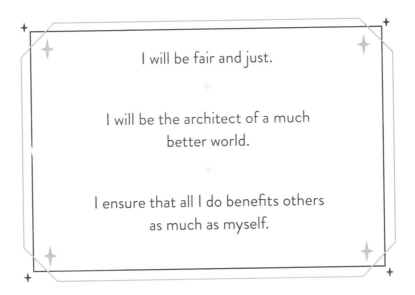

I will be fair and just.

I will be the architect of a much better world.

I ensure that all I do benefits others as much as myself.

Exercise: bringing in balance

Reflect on the areas of your life that may be unbalanced. Think about whether you might need more yin (feminine) or yang (masculine) energies in those areas to bring balance.

If you require more yin, slow down, wear brighter, softer clothing, and focus on sensitivity and emotion.

Embrace your femininity by taking the time to notice your emotions and understand that they're a helpful signal for what's going on in your life right now, rather than a sign of weakness.

If you require more yang, assert yourself more, wear stronger, bolder colours and express yourself with courage and a sense of adventure.

Yang energy is organized and focused and you can tap into it by becoming more organized with lists, a diary or a planner.

Angel Numbers

Angel numbers are a repetitive sequence, or double numbers that repeatedly appear in random places. They are one way that angels make their presence known, perhaps when wanting to communicate a divine message. For example, if you look at the time and it's 10.10 or 21.21, or you notice that a particular number has reappeared on a vehicle number plate, buses or even bills in a restaurant, these numbers could indicate angelic ways of communicating that have turned up to guide you.

Angels are spiritual messengers employed by the universe to communicate with you, and archangels are guardians of humanity and the heavenly realms. Each archangel and angel is associated with a specific number and calling on them will increase their ability to help you. Calling on the angels gives them permission to guide, help and support you – sometimes just feeling their energy surrounding us is enough to soothe and heal. The angels go beyond masculine and feminine principles and in fact embody both, so try not to get too caught up in the traditional male and female connotations arising from their names.

I always pay attention to double numbers and reduce them to one for the message. For example, if you see 33 repeating – perhaps the time is 03.03 when you wake up – this would be reduced to the number 6. But if you then notice repetitive numbers at any point in the day and see 33 somewhere else, as one of the three master numbers (see page 16), then that double number is most certainly a message of importance. When double numbers frequently show themselves to you, this usually means that you are altogether on the right track and can be taken as a message from the cosmos that you are in alignment with the universe and that angels are surrounding you.

Exercise: connect with your angelic message

Angels walk among us and they work in subtle ways – often through other beings – to lift our spirits and guide us. Close your eyes, breathe deeply and say, 'Angels, I give you permission to walk with me, to work with me and to make your presence known.' Now imagine being surrounded by light and breathe that light into your whole being.

1. Create an angel numbers journal and keep it by your bed, or with you when you're out, recording double numbers when you spot them.

2. Perhaps 10.10 reveals itself repeatedly, such as the time you have to catch a train, or the time is 10.10 and you have ten unread messages.

3. The number 10, for example, is about commitments, so the angels are asking you to

review yours. Sit down in a quiet space and think about the following questions: Are they healthy? Sustainable? Do you need to make or break commitments? Or perhaps a new one is winging its way to you.

4. If you have a double number, you may need to reduce it to a single digit if there is no immediate correlation for you with the original double-digit number. Whichever divination method you use, the angels are trying hard to be heard, so slow down and try to tune in to their subtlety.

5. If you spot a couple of 10s, you could add them together: 10 + 10 = 20, reducing to one number. In this case the double number reduces to 2, which is the number belonging to angel Raphael who is widely believed to bring healing energy to any situation. Search Raphael out online for more insight and call on him throughout your daily routine.

Angel Numbers and Their Archangels

1: Archangel Michael

Michael is associated with the number 1. When 1 reveals itself to you repetitively, he is asking you to be brave and courageous in the choices you make. Assertion and gentleness are a supreme blend that overcome fear and aggression in all its forms.

> I call on Archangel Michael to protect me as I stand in my power and grow towards the light; may truth be my shield.

2: Archangel Raphael

The number 2 is associated with Raphael, who is the ultimate defender of the gentle divine feminine energy that exists in every human being. If you look at the digit you'll see how 2 bows its head with humility, yet remains firmly grounded and balanced. If number 2 reveals itself to you several times, it's a prompt to embrace the gentle healing and effective power of the divine feminine.

> I call on Archangel Raphael and the healing power of the divine feminine to surround me, my home and my life.

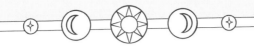

Exercise: attuning to your angel number

1. Visualize the resplendence of your angel by your side and its number surrounding your life.

2. Recall their power regularly and call on them to help you assert your will without aggression.

3. Embrace both assertion and logic, creativity and intuition. This enhances both critical and creative thinking which allows subtle messages to be received and deciphered.

4. Close your eyes, take deep breaths, and imagine yourself surrounded by angels, free from fear; fearless, brave and bold, just like them.

3: Archangel Gabriel

The number 3 is associated with Archangel Gabriel, who is also known as the holy and heavenly messenger. Seeing the number 3 in a repetitive sequence indicates visions and signs of communication from the universe that will help you align with your higher purpose.

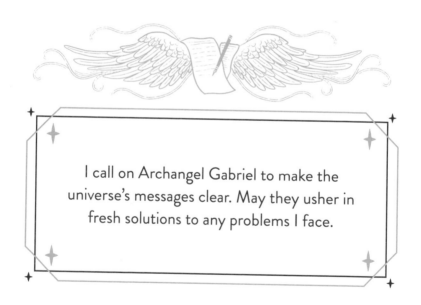

I call on Archangel Gabriel to make the universe's messages clear. May they usher in fresh solutions to any problems I face.

4: Archangel Uriel

Known as the angel of knowledge and wisdom, if number 4 repeatedly shows up as a double number you are being asked by Uriel to seek out knowledge before you make any decisions that may have long-term ramifications in your life.

I call upon the wisdom of Archangel Uriel to educate and awaken my whole being to the possibilities that await.

Exercise: making a pact with your angel

Make a pact with your angel to gain knowledge.

Promise to read (or listen) to at least one chapter a day of a book that will inform, educate and enhance your intelligence, helping your brilliance to shine through.

Visit a bookstore and locate the Philosophy or Spirituality section. Close your eyes and ask the angels to guide your choice towards a book that will enhance your knowledge.

Now reach for a book, buy it and read a chapter every night. Make notes in the book of words or paragraphs that resonate with you.

Reflect on the reasons that these words resonate with you. What do they relate to in your life? What do these words say about you?

5: Archangel Selaphiel

Selaphiel is the archangel of prayers, who also helps us to break the chain of harmful addictions, either our own or of those around us. Seeing the number 5 will signify a need to reassess your behaviour. Also known as a music lover, Selaphiel encourages you to bring the joyous energy of music into your life.

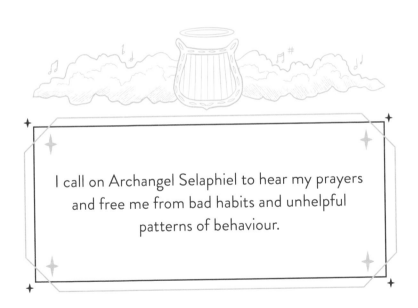

I call on Archangel Selaphiel to hear my prayers and free me from bad habits and unhelpful patterns of behaviour.

Exercise: purifying your life with help from the angels

Close your eyes and imagine a more melodic life. Listen to some beautiful music and note how it makes you feel.

Try searching for 'calming' classical music even if you don't usually listen to it. Most classical music has a really high vibration that produces dopamine (the high-pleasure, anti-stress hormone).

Now make a record of your appreciation for all answered prayers, however small. Gratitude will increase the flow of abundance in your life and more of your prayers will be heard and answered.

Vow to free yourself from toxic people, habits and situations. Ask the angels to help you with this and to make their presence known.

6: Archangel Jehudiel

Jehudiel is the angel of service, helping us to recognize the blessings that are found when we complete acts that benefit others. Associated with 6, Jehudiel also reduces envy whenever it rears its ugly head and empowers us to develop our self-esteem.

I am ready to spread my wings and ascend.
I will not allow envy (my own or others')
to hold me back.

7: Archangel Jophiel

Jophiel (also known as Dina) is the angel of beauty and harmony, overseeing our thoughts to ensure that they are positive and supportive, and helping us to develop into beautiful souls that live harmoniously with others. When you notice double numbers making 7, Jophiel also helps to heal rifts and arguments that may separate us from loved ones or from experiencing the enchantment of life.

My thoughts, words and actions reflect
my own beautiful heart and soul.

8: Archangel Metatron

Metatron teaches us how to use our power as a force for good and also records our choices in the book of life – also known as the Akashic Records. When the number 8 results from your double numbers, he advises us to check our motivation before we say or do anything and encourages us to make sage choices that assist our soul's journey.

I use my intention and power as a force for good and always make wise choices.

Exercise: deciphering your angels' messages

Numerology doesn't encourage the practice of surrendering your own intuition – it is in fact a way to encourage you to use it. Try this exercise if you are repeatedly seeing reoccurring numbers.

1. Find a quiet, uninterrupted space. The more you get used to doing this, the easier it will be to achieve this almost anywhere.

2. Close your eyes and take deep breaths until your mind is calm. Visualize the numbers you have been seeing.

3. Keep breathing restoratively and wait for subtle messages or images from your angels to form in your mind.

9: Archangel Jeremiel

Jeremiel is the angel of visions and dreams; when we call on him, we realize Jeremiel is on hand to support us as we develop our own innate intuition and insight. If your angel number is 9, pay attention to your dreams and the feelings you have when you call upon Jeremial to guide you towards clarity.

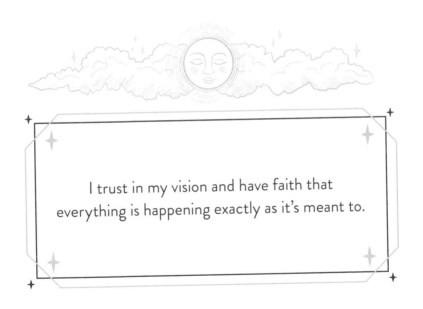

I trust in my vision and have faith that everything is happening exactly as it's meant to.

10: Archangel Chamuel

Chamuel oversees all earthly commitments and partnerships, helps us to form the right relationships and brings romance into our lives. Called up by the number 10, Chamuel believes that only love is real and all else is merely an illusion.

The only thing that is real is love.
I embody love in all its glory and
attract blessed unions.

11: Archangel Zadkiel

Zadkiel offers us to the key to freedom. By the power of the number 11, he guides us to forgive ourselves and those who have wronged us, and calls forth our compassion which enables us to release harsh judgements and frees us from the imprisonment of grudges or regret.

I am free from harmful lower vibrations, and I embrace the courage to live with an open heart.

12: Archangel Sandalphon

Sandalphon oversees our faith and spiritual practice. If you repeatedly see number 12, this is a sign to call on him to help you strengthen your own practice and connection to the benevolent energy of the universe. This angel and number guide you to find the right teachers in life.

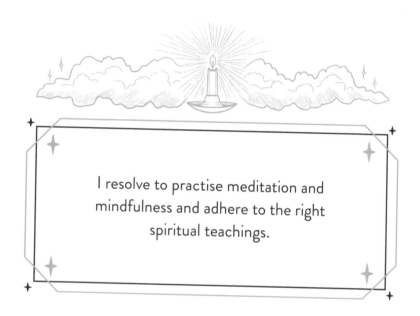

I resolve to practise meditation and mindfulness and adhere to the right spiritual teachings.

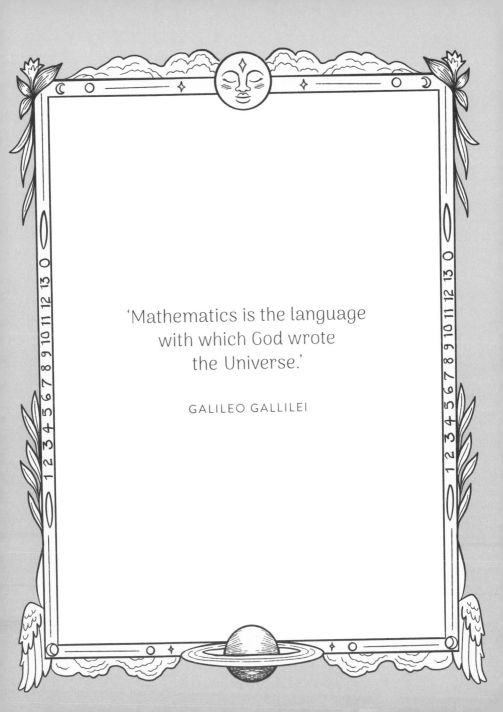

'Mathematics is the language
with which God wrote
the Universe.'

GALILEO GALLILEI

Birthday Numbers

Your birthday number is one of the core numbers that influence you throughout your life and is taken only from the date in the month that you were born on. It's the only type of number in numerology that you don't reduce to one single digit. This is because numerologists believe that your birthday number holds its own very unique meaning and has its own vibration.

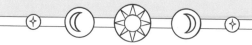

Exercise: preparing yourself

1. Before calculating your birthday number, prepare yourself so you are able to comprehend the messages on a deeper level.

2. Turn your phone off for a little while so you are not disturbed.

3. Sit quietly and close your eyes. Take several deep breaths.

4. Recite the following mantra to prepare yourself: 'As I take these deep breaths, I become calm and the gentle messages of the universe become clearer.'

Day 1

You require freedom, autonomy and independence. When you are at your best you may be charismatic, dynamic, progressive and loyal. When you're not, you may be overly prideful, egotistical and boastful. Ultimately, you are kind, confident and sensitive.

Day 2

You are creative, intuitive and sensitive to the needs of others, especially family members. When you're not quite your usual confident self, you may be overly concerned with the opinions of others, easily hurt and controlling. When in your power you are warm, gentle and charming.

Day 3

You are easy-going and extremely loving. On bad days, you may be insecure and jealous of others. You are likely to be innately talented, inspirational and an incredible source of support to others.

Day 4

You are ambitious, pragmatic and determined. You are more than likely to be extremely hardworking and have the ability to get things done. You are tenacious in all your pursuits, faithful, honest and open-hearted. When you lack trust you can be controlling, stubborn and secretive.

Day 5

You cherish freedom, and you are enthusiastic and willing to take risks that have the potential to enliven your life. You also have excellent attention to detail. Adversely, you can be foolhardy and extravagant.

Day 6

You are caring and take responsibility seriously. You have a compassionate nature which usually means you have good friends and attract others easily. At your best, you are humanitarian and altruistic. When not working with your natural skills, you are a busybody who interferes too much.

Exercise: birthday number ritual

1. On the numbered day you were born (of any month), go outside and find a grassy space.

2. Take off your shoes and feel your connection to the earth below you.

3. Close your eyes and breathe deeply. Thank the universe for your precious birth.

4. Recite the following mantra: 'I am alive, I welcome in the new day and for all I have and will have, I give thanks.'

Day 7

This indicates someone with a strong sense of self and determination. If you are feeling insecure, you can lose sight of the bigger picture. When you are living your best life, you are a discerning perfectionist who dedicates time and thought to other people, and indeed to all your endeavours.

Day 8

You are a powerful person with much potential to achieve. If you are not operating on a high vibration, you are overly ambitious and desire to dominate in your field, and life in general. At best, you are generous, have excellent business acumen, and your organization and executional skills hold the key to success.

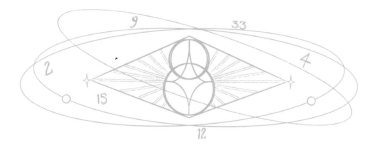

Day 9

Being born on this day of the month indicates a cultured person with a skill for languages. You tend to be well travelled, as well as a seeker of spiritual truth. You are intuitive, creative and extremely kind. Negatively, you may be self-righteous, yet feel inferior to others.

Day 10

You are someone who has leadership capabilities and usually climbs high in life after working hard to get there. You are self-motivated, thoughtful and creative. When not at your best, you can be harsh with others and overly concerned with your own success and material gain.

Day 11

This date indicates a special person (11 is a master number) who is spiritual, empathetic and enthusiastic towards life and people in general. You are dedicated to helping others and speaking the truth. You also have a tendency to be impractical and a little haughty in nature.

Day 12

You have a brilliant mind, faith in your ideas and abilities, and are disciplined and cooperative. When you feel disempowered or unconfident, you're unfocused and fail to finish what you start.

Day 13

You are a highly sensitive and creative person who has the power to turn original ideas into tangible ways of earning a living. You work hard to create abundance and express your individuality well. If you are not working to become the best version of yourself, you may struggle to make commitments and detach from your emotions.

Exercise: helping loved ones

1. Calculate the birthday numbers of friends or loved ones. Pop a note in your diary to wish them well on their day.

2. On that day send them a happy birthday message with the definition of their day from this book (though only send them the words you feel will help them – cross out any that don't ring true).

3. Wish them a wonderful day and remind them how loved they are by you and the universe.

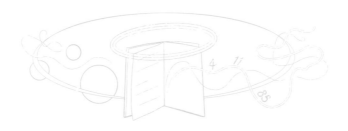

Day 14

You are sensitive, show great discernment and possess strong analytical skills. You are perceptive and have the ability to create success for yourself and others. If you become too self-occupied you may be ungrateful and dissatisfied no matter how much you have achieved.

Day 15

You are artistic and creative. You take great pride in your family and work to ensure your home is harmonious. You also have the ability to learn new things and earn a living in interesting ways. When not at your best you lack focus and can be prone to not finishing the new things you start.

Day 16

You are usually extremely family-orientated with a caring nature, as well as being artistic, hardworking, kind and responsible. If you're not in flow you can be a separatist who cares only for specific groups and you can be hard-headed with your opinions, which may not always be rooted in fact.

Day 17

You have a tendency to be reserved and thoughtful, but show a natural flair for business, and analysis in general. You are strong and have the ability to be a high achiever. If you have not worked on yourself very much, you can be critical and untrusting.

Day 18

You are brave, hardworking and smart. You have a kind heart and always find the right words to help others – perhaps even empowering them. The unattractive side of your number means you sometimes don't give enough thought to feelings of others, and can be argumentative and tactless.

Day 19

You are progressive and care deeply for those less fortunate than you. You are independent, driven and a force to be reckoned with. On the flip side, you may be competitive and egotistic.

Day 20

You are considerate and sensitive to the plights and feelings of others. You also have the ability to be extremely creative and are capable of achieving great things when you set your mind to it. On a not so positive note, you can be indecisive and easily manipulated by those with their own agendas.

Day 21

You are a dynamic person with many friends and connections that are often influential. Charming and loving, you are able to form lasting unions. On the flip side, you can be stubborn, require validation and are fixed in your opinions.

Day 22

Your unique ability to blend logic with intuition gives you great potential to make a positive contribution to society. If you are not careful, you may waste your talents and focus too much on personal and material gain.

Day 23

As a trustworthy and honest person, you are blessed with a sunny disposition. You are loyal, offering sage advice and support to friends and loved ones when required. You may also be noncommittal and impatient.

Day 24

You are an optimistic person, reliable and trustworthy. You are forgiving, hardworking and have a strong moral compass, which gives you an ethical approach to life. On the downside, you have the tendency to be judgemental and hold grudges.

Day 25

You are a fair and intuitive person with sound judgement. You are able to use your imagination to solve problems for yourself and others but tend to be a perfectionist. On bad days, you can be defensive and moody.

Day 26

You are powerful and persuasive, often holding positions of influence. You have the ability to motivate others, make lofty plans and achieve your goals. In pursuit of these goals, you can sometimes be domineering and unforgiving.

Day 27

You love adventure and value autonomy. You are great company, an avid traveller and great at communicating with people from all walks of life. If you lose sight of your natural abilities, you can be indecisive and fickle.

Day 28

You are an assertive and confident person who is determined to succeed. You know your own mind, display sound judgement and a strong sense of direction in life. You may also become prideful and tend to be arrogant.

Day 29

In your flow, you are refreshingly unconventional yet use common sense to guide you and your decisions. If you fail to develop a strong mindset, you may depend too much on others and fear using your own intuition.

Day 30

You are sociable, caring and compassionate, and happiest when conversing with people from all walks of life. On a not so positive note, you may be too concerned with yourself, and be lazy and impatient.

Day 31

You tend to be blessed with good fortune, are charismatic, well-liked and appreciative of any good luck and opportunities that come your way. If you lack focus, you ignore signs and red flags that can sometimes lead you in the wrong direction.

Communicating With
Your Higher Self

You have reached the end of this book and the beginning of a whole new path. This path has the potential to unlock the sacred from the seemingly mundane. It helps you to unveil hidden messages from the universe that are ripe for interpretation.

Keep this book with you so that you may dip in and out of it and refer to it when you feel you need a little help or guidance to stay in tune with the vibrations around you. But never lose touch with your own intuition – this is where the voices of angels speak to you and the universe holds space for you to let your dreams manifest. Numbers are a divine and ancient way that help us to understand the messages and inspiration that are all around us, every day – there to communicate with us, our soul and our higher selves.

May you be happy, and may your path be illuminated by light.

About the author

Carolyne Faulkner has been named 'Britain's coolest astrologer' by *Forbes*, *Grazia* and the *Telegraph*. She was the first and only in-house astrologer for the Soho House Group for over ten years and regularly holds events in their houses around the world. She created and launched the concept of Dynamic Astrology™ in 2014 – a unique blend of astrology, energetic awareness, and mind mastery. Carolyne uses numerology and the movements of the planets to empower others to practise self-reflection and improvement.
www.dynamicastrology.com

About the artist

Anna Stead is an illustrator based in the beautiful North Cotswolds, England. She draws inspiration from nature, legend, history, folklore, literature, folk art and the mythic arts. She has a background in medieval studies and is a lover of fantasy literature. She can be found with a cat in her lap, playing video games or sketching on her iPad whenever she gets a chance.
www.thistlemoon.co.uk